Piranha

KIDS EXPLORE!

Thanks for checking out the Kids Explore!Series. Please note:All Rights Reserved. No part of this publication may be reproduced in any form or by any means, including scanning, photocopying, or otherwise without prior written permission of the copyright holder. Copyright © 2014

Piranha

The Piranha is a fish with big teeth. It is best known for its ferociousness. The word Piranha means, fish tooth in the Amazon. There are around 60 types of Piranha. They will live in large groups called, schools. Schools of Piranha can number up to 1,000 individual fish. Let's explore the world of the Piranha. In this book we will discover all sorts of new and interesting things. Read on to be wowed and amazed. But beware, this fish can be a bit snappy!

Where in the World?

Did you know the Piranha is a freshwater fish? Piranhas can be found in rivers in South America. These fast moving rivers run through the jungles. Piranhas have been found in almost every country in South America. The Piranha has also been spotted in some southern US states, as well.

The Body of a Piranha

Did you know the Piranha can grow quite large? Piranhas can grow to be around 17 inches long (43 centimeters). They are tear-drop in shape and have a dull greyish green color on their bodies. Some have bright red bellies. The Piranha's eyes are close to its large mouth.

The Teeth

Did you know the Piranha has razor-sharp teeth? This fish has a row of teeth on both its upper and lower jaws. These teeth are very close together and triangular. They are very sharp and blade-like. The Piranha uses its sharp teeth to rip into its prey. These teeth make the Piranha a very scary fish.

The Piranha Has a Special Ability

Did you know a school of Piranha can eat super-fast? When a large group of hungry Piranhas all begin to eat, it is called a, frenzy. It would only take seconds for a school of Piranha to eat an entire cow. This is why the Piranha are feared throughout the jungles of South America.

What a Piranha Eats

Did you know Piranhas do not just eat meat? This is called; an omnivore. The Piranha will dine on snails, insects, fish and aquatic plants. Sometimes, the Piranha will eat larger animals or birds that may fall into the water. In the dry season when food is hard to find, the Piranha are more likely to attack people.

The Resting Piranha

Did you know the Piranha takes a break from eating? When Piranhas are not eating, they will swim around in schools. These fish are not always on the attack. If you were to see Piranha in an aquarium, you may think it is just an ordinary fish.

Enemies of the Piranha

Did you know the Piranha has natural enemies? Even though this fish has sharp teeth, it still has natural predators. Large animals such as the river dolphin, turtles, bigger fish and crocodiles will dine on the Piranha. Some bird species will also swoop down and catch Piranha, as well.

Piranha Mom and Dad

Did you know both the mom and dad Piranha protect their young? Mom Piranha will lay around 5,000 eggs at one time. She does this is in a still lagoon from April to May. Because both parents protect the eggs, almost all of the babies will hatch out. That's a lot of Piranha!

Baby Piranhas

Did you know baby Piranha are born very small? Baby Piranhas only measure about 1.5 inches long (3.8 centimeters). Baby Piranhas eat most anything. This can include small snails, plants and even the fins of larger fish. The Piranha babies grow very quickly. This helps keep them from getting eaten by larger animals.

Piranha and People

Did you know people have used the Piranha for many things? In some cultures the Piranha has been caught for its meat. The teeth of the Piranha were also used to make tools and weapons from. Today the Piranha can be seen in many large zoo aquariums. Some people even keep them as pets.

Piranhas as Pets

Did you know lots of places will not let you keep Piranhas as pets? These fish do not make good pets. They grow very quickly and need a very large place to live. Piranhas will attack each other in a fish tank. For this reason they need to be kept in a small group. Piranhas can also be very expensive to feed.

Life of a Piranha

Did you know most Piranha can live a long life? Piranhas can live to be from 8 to 10 years-old. This is probably due to their vicious nature. Once Piranhas have their big sharp teeth, they can protect themselves. However, not all Piranhas are mean. Some are peaceful and just eat seeds and veggies.

The Black Piranha

Did you know the Black Piranha has the most powerful bite of all Piranha? This Piranha is black in color. Its sharp teeth pack a real bite. For its size, its bite is compared to that of a T-Rex! This fish only eats meat. However, they are rare and hard to find in nature.

Red-Bellied Piranha

Did you know the Red-Bellied Piranha is very common? This Piranha has a bright-red belly. It is found in the Amazon Basin in South America. This Piranha is the one kept as a pet. It is less vicious than its cousins. It will eat meat, plants and dead fish.

Quiz

Question 1: Where is the Piranha found?

Answer 1: In most of the countries in South America

Question 2: What does Piranha mean in Amazon?

Answer 2: Fish tooth

Question 3: How big can a Piranha grow?

Answer 3: Around 17 inches long (43 centimeters)

Question 4: What is the Piranha known for?

Answer 4: Its razor-sharp teeth

Question 5: When a group of Piranha are all eating very quickly, what is it called?

Answer 5: A feeding frenzy

Thank you for checking out another title from Kids Explore! Make sure to check out Amazon.com for many other great books.

Made in the USA
Columbia, SC
23 November 2018